To my poppa,
Don Sturkey,
who always believed in me
and who taught me what
extraordinary is all about.

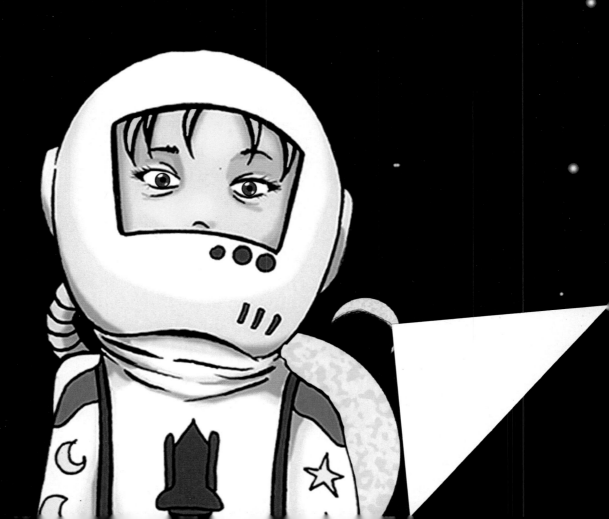

Introduction

Does your child have a friend, family member, or classmate who has Down syndrome? Would you like your child or the children in your classroom to understand more about Down syndrome? Are you looking for an engaging way to start a dialogue about Down syndrome? I wrote this book to solve these challenges.

D is for Down Syndrome is a children's picture book in an ABC format. With delightful illustrations, this book teaches typical traits that many people with Down syndrome share. The book uses child-friendly language and is narrated by a 6-year-old with Down syndrome. *D is for Down Syndrome* provides an entertaining way to start a simple educational discussion about Down syndrome.

I invite you to read this story interactively with your child. You can playfully yell really loud, strike muscle poses, and sign "please" with the child in this story. Encourage discussions of how you or your friends might be like the child in this book. You might compare and contrast how the child in this book is similar or different from a person you know with Down syndrome.

I believe knowledge helps break down barriers and encourages kindness and patience. Helping children understand Down syndrome at a young age is powerful. Reading this book will change the life of your child and the lives of people with Down syndrome that your child meets now and in the future.

D is for Down Syndrome

A Child's View

Published by Gotcha Apps, LLC
1904 ½ Williams St.
Valdosta, GA 31602

Copyright © 2017 Amy E. Sturkey, PT

This book provides general information on Down syndrome. It should not be relied upon as recommending or promoting any specific diagnosis or method of treatment. It is not intended as a substitute for medical advice or for direct diagnosis and treatment of Down syndrome by a qualified physician. Readers who have questions about Down syndrome or its treatment should consult with a physician or other qualified health care professional.

ISBN 10: 0-9981567-2-8

ISBN-13: 978-0-9981567-2-9

Library of Congress Control Number: 2017911435

Cover art and interior artwork by Ikos Ronzkie

Text by Amy E. Sturkey, PT

D is for Down Syndrome

A Child's View

written by
Amy E. Sturkey, PT

illustrated by
Ikos Ronzkie

A is for Able.
Sometimes people look at me and think of all the things I can't do. I have Down syndrome, and I am able to do a lot. I can talk, and walk, and ride a tricycle downhill super fast. I can wiggle. I can giggle. I can give you a little tickle. I hope we can be friends.

B is for BIG!
I am so big. I can jump. I can run.
I can make friends. I can yell really loud.
Ahhhhhhhhh!

C is for Chromosome.

Momma says that's a big word for a teeny tiny thing in all of us. Chromosomes have the plans for how people are made. Most people have 46 chromosomes. I have 47 chromosomes, with an extra copy of chromosome 21, way down deep inside of me. That's why I have Down syndrome.

D is for Down syndrome.
Want to know why I am so fun? Down syndrome
is a part of who I am. It is one of the things that
makes me awesome. I am also a great dancer.
I am super at making faces in the mirror.
Watch this!

E is for Exercise.
My daddy says that it is important for all of us to
exercise. Exercising keeps me healthy and strong.
I love to jump on my trampoline with Daddy.
He says I am going to swim in the summer.
I can't wait!

F is for Face.
Everybody's face is different. My face is different
from yours. My nose, my mouth and my eyes all
fit together differently than yours do.
I am beautiful, just like you!

G is for my Giant personality.
I might not be as tall as you, but I make up for it
in my larger-than-life personality. People say
I can be stubborn… but I call it will power.
Watch out world. Here I come!

H is for Hands.

My hands are probably not as strong as yours. I have trouble writing, cutting with scissors, and getting dressed in the morning. I go to therapy to help me get stronger and stronger.

I is for what I know.
I know after reading my book that you might
want Down syndrome, too. But, you can't catch
it by hanging out with me. The only way you can
get Down syndrome is to be born with it,
like I was.

J is for Joy.
Sometimes I am super
happy, just like you.
I love to laugh and sing.
Sometimes, I feel mad
or sad, but I don't hold
grudges. I live right
here and right now!

K is for Knowing I was made special.
My momma says I have a special mission with
my extra set of plans way down deep inside me.
My life is going to be different from yours. I will
grow, get stronger, and learn. I will be slower than
you. But Momma says that gives us time to enjoy
every step of the way.

L is for Love.
My daddy says that the
most important thing
we do here on Earth is
to love one another.
Love others and let
others love us back.
Daddy says that part
of my plan is the same
as everyone else's.

M is for Muscle power!
I am getting stronger every day.
My muscles are not strung as
tight as yours are, so I have to
work harder for everything I do.
But, the more I do, the stronger
I get! I think you are the
same way too!

N is for Nice.

I hope you can be nice to me.
Sometimes people are mean to me
because I look and talk differently.
It feels bad when people laugh at me.
I like it better when we laugh together.
No bullies please.

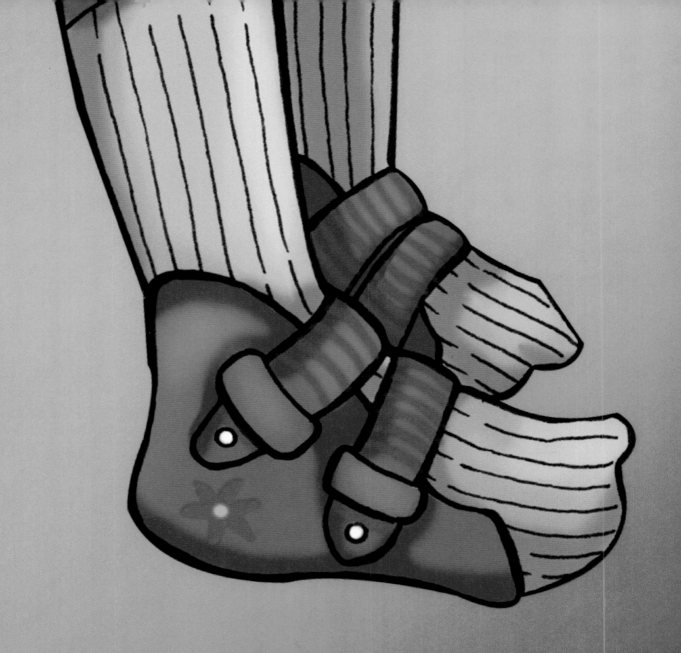

O is for the Orthotics that I wear to help make
my feet strong. I used to wear taller braces.
Now I can wear ones that just go inside my shoes.
One day I'll get rid of them altogether.

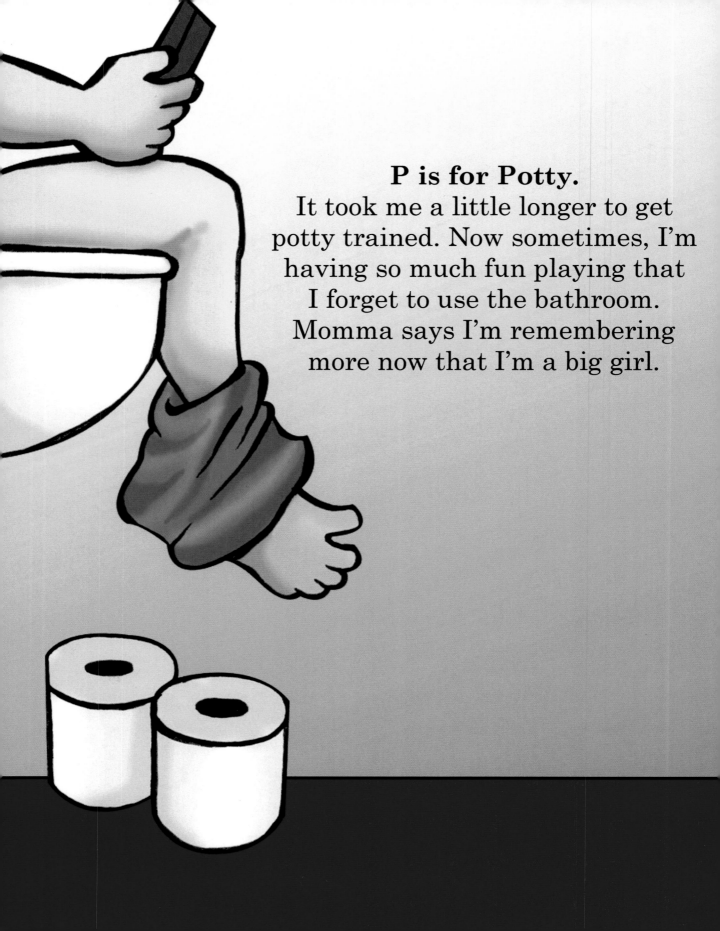

P is for Potty.
It took me a little longer to get potty trained. Now sometimes, I'm having so much fun playing that I forget to use the bathroom. Momma says I'm remembering more now that I'm a big girl.

Q is for NOT Quitting.
My daddy says when something is hard,
I have to keep trying. So right now I am working
hard at climbing stairs with big steps, drawing,
and getting dressed all by myself. I cannot quit.
Maybe you have things that are hard for you to do.
Let me tell you, "Do not Quit!"

R is for Running.
This year, for Special Olympics,
I ran the 50-yard dash. I won a gold medal.
I loved hearing everyone cheer for me!

S is for Signing.

I used signs to learn how to talk. I could say simple things like "More, please," and "Finished," by moving my hands. Do you know how to make those signs? Now I can talk, and my hands don't have to help me.

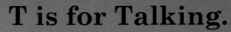

T is for Talking.
I don't always say my words clearly.
I go to a speech therapist to help me learn
how to talk better. My speech therapist is
Ms. Jones. We play fun talking games.

U is for Understanding.
I may not talk as well as you,
but I understand a lot. I don't like it when
people talk to me like I am a baby.
I am 6 years old!

V is for Very different.
No two people with Down syndrome are exactly the same. Some are taller. Some are shorter. Some are faster. Some are slower. Some are great talkers. Others don't talk. We are all different, just like people who don't have Down syndrome!

W is for Walking.
My momma says it took me twice as long to learn to walk. But look at me now! I am winning races!

X is for eXcited.
I am so excited that you know about Down syndrome now. I hope that you and I can be friends.

Y is for You.
You and I can have fun together!
We can play. I can learn from you,
and you can learn from me.
Isn't that how friends should be?

Z is for Zip.
Zip on over here,
and let's get started.
Catch me if you can!

The end.

Consider these 3 requests from a
child with Down Syndrome:

◇◇

3-Step Action Plan

1. Include Me
2. Encourage Me
3. Expect Great Things
   from Me

Other offerings by the author:

◇◇

A is for Autism: A Child's View
Pediatric Physical Therapy Exercises for Abdominals
for Apple and Android

Pediatric Physical Therapy Exercises for Back Extension
for Apple and Android

Pediatric Physical Therapy Exercises for Knee Extension
for Apple and Android

Weekly Blog:
www.pediatricPTexercises.com

Weekly pediatric physical therapy treatment emails:
www.pediatricPTexercises.com

YouTube Channel:
Pediatric Physical Therapy Exercises

Facebook page:
Pediatric Physical Therapy Exercises

Instagram page:
Pediatric PT Exercises

Pinterest page:
amysturkey/pediatric-physical-therapy

About the Illustrator

Ikos Ronzkie is an international graphic designer, book illustrator, and comic artist. She creates fanciful illustrations for advertisements, campaigns, comic books, character designs, book designs and book covers. She has worked as an illustrator with local and international clientele for over 11 years.

She is the illustrator for books including: *A is for Autism, What Babies Do, What Do I Do Well?, The Loosey Goosey Tooth, Princess Superhero Antonia, The Tooth Fairy* and *Willy Nilly Adventures.*

Her clients include international publishers, dollmakers, comic book writers, authors, and picture book writers. She produces *Bayan ng Biyahero Comics* for the Antipolo Star Newspaper for the Rizal and Metro Manila distribution areas. She previously created *Estudyante Blues* for the Living News and Good Education magazine. Independently, she writes and produces her own comics: *Karit, Dalawang Liham, Sulsi* and the webcomics *Hilda Intrimitida.* Ronzkie is the co-founder of IKOS Komiks which strives to promote and explore Philippine culture with visual and literary arts. Their creations are dedicated to work inspired by the Philippine history, myths and legends.

◇◇◇◇◇◇◇◇◇◇◇◇◇◇◇◇◇◇◇◇◇◇◇◇◇◇